# PITTSBURGH
## PIRATES

WITHDRAWN

by Ray Frager

Published by ABDO Publishing Company, 8000 West 78th Street, Edina, Minnesota 55439. Copyright © 2011 by Abdo Consulting Group, Inc. International copyrights reserved in all countries. No part of this book may be reproduced in any form without written permission from the publisher. SportsZone™ is a trademark and logo of ABDO Publishing Company.

Printed in the United States of America,
North Mankato, Minnesota
112010
012011

Editor: Matt Tustison
Copy Editor: Nicholas Cafarelli
Interior Design and Production: Kazuko Collins
Cover Design: Kazuko Collins

**Photo Credits:** Gene J. Puskar/AP Images, cover, 38, 47; AP Images, title, 4, 7, 8, 13, 15, 16, 19, 20, 23, 25, 26, 28, 31, 42 (top, middle, bottom), 43 (top, middle), 44; Mark Rucker/Transcendental Graphics/Getty Images, 10; Leon Algee/AP Images, 32; John Swart/AP Images, 35; Doug Mills/AP Images, 37, 43 (bottom); John Heller/AP Images, 41

**Library of Congress Cataloging-in-Publication Data**
Frager, Ray.
  Pittsburgh Pirates / by Ray Frager.
     p. cm. — (Inside MLB)
  Includes index.
  ISBN 978-1-61714-055-6
  1.  Pittsburgh Pirates (Baseball team—History—Juvenile literature.  I. Title.
  GV975.P5F73 2011
  796.357'640974886—dc22
                          2010038091

# TABLE OF CONTENTS

# CHAPTER 1

# WORLD SERIES DRAMA

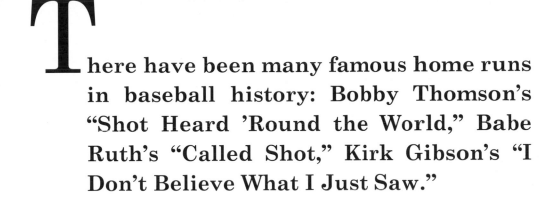

**T**here have been many famous home runs in baseball history: Bobby Thomson's "Shot Heard 'Round the World," Babe Ruth's "Called Shot," Kirk Gibson's "I Don't Believe What I Just Saw."

But many baseball followers believe that it was a Pittsburgh Pirate who hit the most important homer ever.

Bill Mazeroski ended the 1960 World Series with a home run. The only other time a player homered on the final play of a Series occurred in 1993. That year, Joe Carter accomplished the feat for the Toronto Blue Jays. But unlike Carter, whose shot came in Game 6, Mazeroski hit his home run in the final possible game of the Series, Game 7.

How did the Pirates even get to that point? They had gone decades without even a National League (NL) pennant. Their previous World Series appearance had been in 1927.

However, the 1960 team came together in a magical

Pittsburgh fans rush onto the field to greet Bill Mazeroski after he hit a game-winning homer in Game 7 of the World Series on October 13, 1960.

## BILL MAZEROSKI

Though Bill Mazeroski became famous for hitting a home run, what really set him apart was how good he was defensively as a second baseman. Some baseball experts say he was the best fielder ever at the position.

Still, "Maz" kept getting overlooked for the Hall of Fame because he was a much better fielder than he was a hitter. But he finally was voted into the Hall in 2001. Mazeroski was picked by a special group of voters called the Veterans Committee. One of the members of the committee was Yogi Berra, a player for the 1960 Yankees team that lost to the Pirates in the World Series. "I'm glad we elected him. He belongs there," Berra said.

Mazeroski, a native of West Virginia, played his entire big-league career with the Pirates, from 1956 to 1972. He was a seven-time All-Star and won eight Gold Glove Awards for his fielding.

way. Branch Rickey had acquired several of the players years earlier when he was the Pirates' general manager. Rickey, the man responsible for breaking baseball's color barrier with Jackie Robinson and the Brooklyn Dodgers, was gone from Pittsburgh by 1960.

A new general manager, Joe L. Brown, collected the rest of the pieces for the Pirates. It turned out that those pieces fit together well.

Pittsburgh had terrific defense. The infield featured the sure hands of second baseman Mazeroski, shortstop Dick Groat, and third baseman Don Hoak. Bill Virdon and Roberto Clemente were outstanding in the outfield. Clemente possessed a very strong throwing arm.

Vernon Law, who won 20 games and the Cy Young

The Pirates' Bill Mazeroski, shown in 1962, is most famous for his World Series-winning home run in 1960, but the second baseman had a long career with many highlights.

Award as the major leagues' best pitcher, led the pitching staff. It also included Bob Friend, Wilmer "Vinegar Bend" Mizell, and Roy Face.

The Pirates received power hitting from first baseman Dick Stuart. He slugged 23 home runs. The two players who shared the catching job, Smoky Burgess and Hal Smith, combined for 18 homers and 84 runs batted in (RBIs). Stuart and outfielder Bob Skinner each drove in more than 80 runs. Clemente collected 94

Pirates shortstop Dick Groat holds a bat with "325" written on it. Groat was the NL's MVP in 1960 and had a league-best .325 batting average.

RBIs along with a .314 batting average.

Groat was named NL Most Valuable Player (MVP) and won the league batting title with a .325 average. Groat missed most of the last month of the regular season. He suffered a broken wrist when he was hit by a pitch. But substitute Dick Schofield replaced Groat with an MVP-like effort.

In the World Series, the Pirates faced the Yankees. In

the prior 10 years, New York had been in the World Series seven times and won five.

Game 7 went back and forth. The Yankees scored two runs to make it 7–4 in the eighth. But the Pirates came back with five runs in the bottom of the inning to lead 9–7. The Yankees tied it with two runs in the top of the ninth.

Then came the bottom of the ninth. Mazeroski was the leadoff batter that inning. On the second pitch from the Yankees' Ralph Terry, Mazeroski hit a ball to left-center field that just cleared the fence. The Pirates had won the World Series in a most dramatic way.

"As I was heading into second, I saw the umpire down the left-field line waving his arms in a circle and I heard people screaming," Mazeroski said. "Then when I first knew it was out, as I was going into second,

## Famous Call

*Chuck Thompson was one of the radio announcers for Game 7 of the 1960 World Series. Because it was a famous moment, his call of Bill Mazeroski's winning homer has been replayed many times. And so people have heard the mistakes Thompson made over and over. First, he named the wrong pitcher for the Yankees. Then, after Mazeroski's homer, Thompson gave the wrong score: "Ladies and gentlemen, Bill Mazeroski has just hit a one-nothing pitch over the left-field wall to win the 1960 World Series for the Pittsburgh Pirates by a score of 10 to nothing!" Thompson corrected himself and gave the right score.*

all I could think about was, 'We beat the Yankees! We beat the Yankees!'"

Fans poured into downtown Pittsburgh to celebrate. About 300,000 people came out to enjoy the Pirates' championship. It is still the most celebrated moment for a team whose history dates all the way to the 1880s.

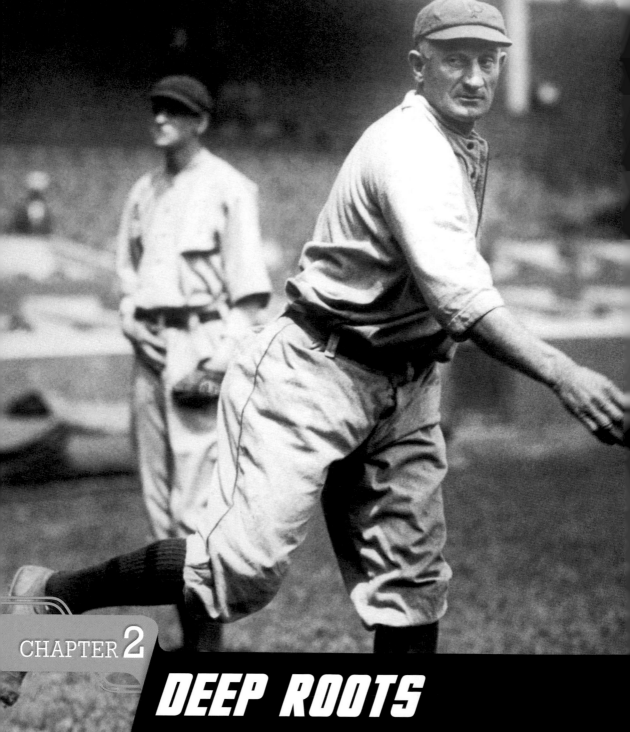

# CHAPTER 2

# DEEP ROOTS

The Pirates' history goes all the way back to the very beginnings of professional baseball. Pittsburgh's first pro team, called the Alleghenys, began playing in 1876. They lasted only a few years. But the second version of the Alleghenys started up in 1882. That is the team that eventually became known as the Pirates in 1891.

The Allegheny Mountains run through the region, and the Allegheny River flows through Pittsburgh.

For the 1887 season, Pittsburgh replaced the Kansas City Cowboys as a franchise in the NL. For its first 13 seasons, the team mostly struggled. In 1890,

## Argh!

*The Pittsburgh baseball team originally was called the Alleghenys. In 1891, the team signed a second baseman named Louis Bierbauer. The Philadelphia Athletics had considered Bierbauer their player. The A's accused the Pittsburgh club of being "pirates." The name stuck.*

Hall of Fame shortstop Honus Wagner warms up for the Pirates in 1915 in New York. Teammate Max Carey is in the background.

## HONUS WAGNER

Though Honus Wagner played his last game for the Pirates in 1917, he is still ranked among baseball's best all-around players by experts. John McGraw, a successful big-league manager in the early 1900s, said of Wagner, "He was the nearest thing to a perfect player no matter where his manager chose to play him."

Wagner mostly played short-stop, though, and was known for getting to almost any ball in his area and then throwing out runners with a strong arm. At a time when the stolen base was a major weapon in baseball, he led the NL in steals five times.

Wagner did not hit many home runs, but those were a rarity in his time. However, he led the NL in batting average eight times and drove in at least 100 runs nine times. Wagner finished with a career batting average of .328.

the squad won 23 games and lost 113.

Things changed in 1900. The NL decided to cut its number of teams from 12 to eight. Barney Dreyfuss had owned the Louisville team. It was being shut down. Dreyfuss became owner of the Pirates. Just as importantly, Dreyfuss brought 14 of his Louisville players with him.

Among the important Louisville players who became Pirates were a pair of future Hall of Famers—outfielder/manager Fred Clarke and pitcher Rube Waddell. But none of the players who arrived from Louisville was more important than short-stop Honus Wagner.

Wagner is considered by many baseball experts to be one of the greatest players in major league history. He was one of the first players elected

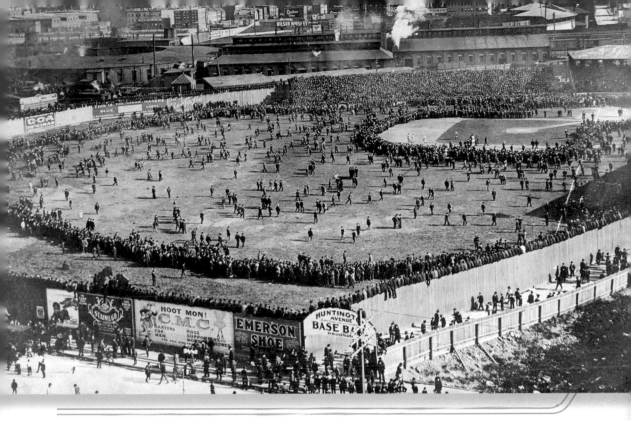

The Huntington Avenue Baseball Grounds are shown on October 1, 1903, in Boston, Massachusetts, before Game 1 of the first World Series. The Pirates defeated the host Americans 7–3 in the game but lost the series.

to the Baseball Hall of Fame. Wagner won eight NL batting titles, had outstanding speed, and was considered the best-fielding shortstop in the game.

The season after the Louisville crew came to Pittsburgh, the Pirates started a streak of three straight NL pennants. After the third, in 1903, Dreyfuss earned the title "Father of

the World Series." He agreed to a championship series against the Boston Americans (later the Red Sox), winners of the American League (AL) pennant. There was a feeling against playing such a series by some in the NL. The NL was more established.

But Dreyfuss said, "Sure, we'll play them if they want to

meet us." Thus was born the World Series.

The Series came to use a best-of-seven format. But that first one was best of nine. The first team to win five games would be the champion. Boston featured the pitching of the great Cy Young. The Americans won the title, five games to three.

The Pirates returned to the World Series in 1909. This time they faced the Detroit Tigers. That meant a matchup between Wagner and Detroit's Ty Cobb. They were considered the best players in the game.

The Series, by now using a best-of-seven format, came down to Game 7. The Pirates won 8–0 thanks to a shutout by Babe Adams. Wagner had a much better Series than Cobb.

## Nice Collectible

*A card that shows the Pirates' Honus Wagner became the most expensive baseball card of all time. The rare card was printed in 1909 by a cigarette company. Wagner opposed smoking, so he asked the company to stop printing the cards. That limited the number produced, making them more valuable. One of the cards sold for $2.8 million in 2007.*

The Pirates' shortstop batted .333, while Cobb hit .231.

In 1909, the Pirates also opened a new ballpark, Forbes Field. It would be their home for 61 years.

After that championship season, the Pirates went into a pennant drought. They did not return to the World Series until 1925.

This rare baseball card of Pirates legend Honus Wagner has sold for as much as $2.8 million. Ex-hockey great Wayne Gretzky once owned a copy.

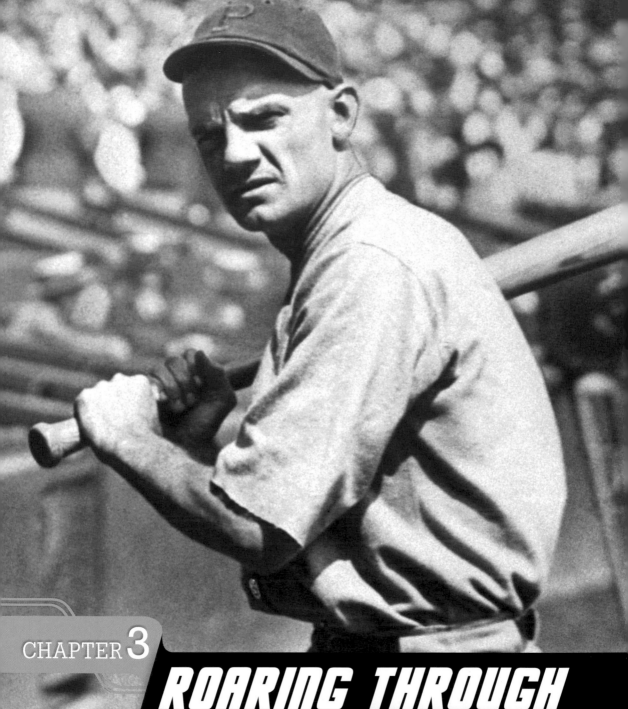

# CHAPTER 3

# ROARING THROUGH THE '20S

The 1920s were a glorious time for the Pirates. Several future Hall of Fame players joined the team. Pittsburgh enjoyed a winning season each year during that decade. The Pirates won the NL pennant twice.

One of those future Hall of Famers was shortstop Rabbit Maranville. Despite his fine play, Maranville was not a favorite of manager Bill McKechnie. Maranville and first baseman Charlie Grimm went out on the town and enjoyed themselves too much for the manager's taste. Before the 1925 season, Maranville and Grimm were traded to the Chicago Cubs. In return, the Pirates received three players. They included first baseman George Grantham and pitcher Vic Aldridge. Grantham hit .326 that season, and Aldridge won 15 games.

The Pirates won the NL pennant in 1925 and headed to the World Series against the Washington Senators. The Senators featured

Outfielder Max Carey was one of many Hall of Fame players for the Pirates in the 1920s. He helped the team win the 1925 World Series.

fireball-throwing pitcher Walter Johnson. Trailing three games to one, Pittsburgh made history. The Pirates became the first team to come back from such a deficit to win a World Series.

The champion Pirates had a load of hitters. The overall team batting average was .307. Kiki Cuyler, an outfielder in his second major league season, hit .357, scored 144 runs, and drove in 102. Another outfielder, Max Carey, was at the end of his career. He was in his 15th big-league season. But Carey hit .343 and led the NL in stolen bases with 46, even though he was 35 years old.

The Pirates had another of the all-time greats at third base, Pie Traynor. As a fielder with quick hands, Traynor was known for robbing batters of doubles by snagging balls headed down the third-base line. He ended up playing 17 seasons with Pittsburgh. He had a lifetime batting average of .320 and hit over .300 in 10 seasons. Traynor totaled at least 100 RBIs in seven seasons.

After dropping to third place in 1926, the Pirates returned to the World Series in 1927. The team had added two strong-hitting outfielders in brothers Paul and Lloyd Waner. Paul, 24 years old, hit .380, and Lloyd, 21, hit .355. Traynor batted .342 with 106 RBIs.

## Rainy Day

*The seventh game of the 1925 World Series between the Pirates and the Washington Senators was played in rainy and foggy conditions in Pittsburgh. Poor visibility might have had something to do with the umpires' ruling on the Pirates' winning hit. Kiki Cuyler hit a bases-loaded double down the right-field line in the eighth inning. The Senators claimed it was a foul ball. But the umpire ruled it fair. The Pirates won 9–7 and captured the title.*

Third baseman Pie Traynor fields the ball at spring training in March 1932 in California. The Hall of Famer was a Pirate from 1920 to 1937.

In the World Series, though, the Pirates had to face the mighty New York Yankees. Their 1927 team might have been the best ever. The Yankees' hitting lineup, featuring Babe Ruth and Lou Gehrig, was so powerful that it was known as Murderer's Row. New York won the Series in four straight games.

That World Series was to be the Pirates' last for 33 years.

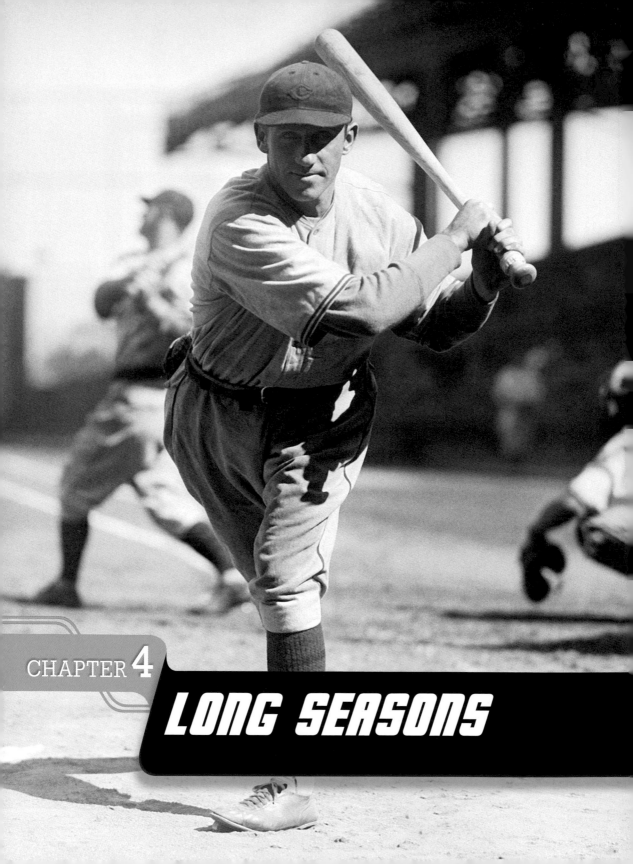

# CHAPTER 4

# LONG SEASONS

The 1930s began an era of change for the Pirates. It was not a change for the better. Before the decade started, the team made an ill-fated move that would affect it for years to come.

After their pennant-winning 1927 season, the Pirates traded outfielder Kiki Cuyler. He had disagreed with manager Donie Bush's decision to bat him second in the lineup. In that spot, Cuyler would have fewer chances to drive in runs. Cuyler and Bush soon got into an argument. The manager put Cuyler on the bench.

Cuyler did not appear in the 1927 World Series. The Pirates then traded him to the Chicago Cubs for two players who ended up doing little. Cuyler went on to continue a Hall of Fame career.

In 1932, owner Barney Dreyfuss, who had built the Pirates into a winning team, died of pneumonia. His widow and son-in-law took over the team.

Though they did not win another pennant, the Pirates

Outfielder Kiki Cuyler, shown in 1932 with the Cubs, was a star with Pittsburgh before he was traded after the 1927 season. The Pirates would not win the NL pennant for more than three decades after the swap.

fielded some competitive teams during the 1930s. They finished second three times between 1932 and 1938.

Perhaps the most distinctive part of the Pirates' lineup in those years were the two brothers who ranked among baseball's best hitters. They also had most distinctive nicknames: Paul "Big Poison" Waner and Lloyd "Little Poison" Waner. Both are in the Hall of Fame.

Despite the "Big" in his nickname, Paul Waner was not a large man. He was 5-foot-8 and about 150 pounds. But that did not stop him when it came to hitting. He had a career batting average of .333. After 20 major league seasons, 15 of them with Pittsburgh, he retired with more than 3,000 hits.

Lloyd Waner was about the same size as his older brother and was also an outfielder. He played 18 years in the majors, all but one with the Pirates. Lloyd Waner had a career batting average of .316. He hit over .300 for all but five of his 17 seasons in Pittsburgh.

The Pirates seemed to be headed for another pennant in 1938. Pittsburgh led the NL by

## Babe's Last Blasts

*The last home run of Babe Ruth's career came in Pittsburgh. Fittingly for baseball's great slugger, he did it in dramatic fashion. Ruth, who had left the New York Yankees, was finishing up with the Boston Braves. At 40, he was no longer the terrific player of his prime. But in Pittsburgh that day, he was a star on the field for one last time. Ruth hit three home runs on May 25, 1935, against the Pirates. Ruth's last home run, number 714 for his career, cleared the 86-foot-high stands in right field and left Forbes Field. He was the first batter to hit a homer out of the park to right. A newspaper story described how "Pirate players stood in their tracks to watch the flight of the ball." Five days later, Ruth played his last game.*

Pirates outfielders Paul Waner, *left*, and his brother Lloyd pose in 1940. Both would be enshrined in the Baseball Hall of Fame.

seven games heading into the last month of the season. The club was so confident that it was going to win the NL title that it built a new press box at Forbes Field to hold the reporters who would cover the World Series. But the lead was down to two with seven games left in the season. And then the Pirates went to Chicago and lost first place to the Cubs, who won the pennant instead.

Over the next 20 seasons, the Pirates had only six winning years. They finished last or next to last 10 times. Their worst season was 1952, when the Pirates had a record of 42–112. Some experts rank it among the worst teams ever.

Still, the Pirates featured some great players during this time. One of them was another shortstop who was a tremendous hitter. Arky Vaughan played 14 seasons in the major leagues, 10 with Pittsburgh, from 1932 to 1941. Vaughan had a lifetime batting average of .318. He never hit lower than .300 for the Pirates.

Starting in 1946, the Pirates added another tremendous hitter, one who put fans in the stands. Outfielder Ralph Kiner put on home-run displays year after year.

In Kiner's second season, 1947, the Pirates lost 92 games. But they still set a team attendance record, drawing almost 1.3 million fans to Forbes Field. Why? Fans wanted to see Kiner hit home runs.

"It was amazing," fellow Pirate Frank Gustine, an infielder, said. "If Ralph batted in the eighth, it seemed like the whole place would get up and leave. But if there was a chance he would bat in the ninth, nobody left."

Kiner hit at least 40 homers five times in his seven full

## Almost Perfect

*On May 26, 1959, Harvey Haddix pitched an amazing 12 perfect innings for the Pirates against the Braves in Milwaukee. He did not allow a single runner to reach first base by any means—hit, walk, or error. But the Pirates did not score any runs. In the 13th inning, Haddix finally allowed Braves base runners and Milwaukee scored to win the game 1–0. For all of his perfect innings of pitching, all Haddix ended up with was a loss. After his wonderful performance, Haddix had offers to appear on television shows. But he turned them down. "He was overwhelmed by the attention," his wife said. "At heart, he was just a farm boy who loved picking corn more than anything else."*

Pirates slugger Ralph Kiner, shown in 1947, set a record by leading the NL in home runs seven seasons in a row, from 1946 to 1952.

years in Pittsburgh. He also drove in more than 100 runs in five of those years. The Pirates, who were looking to have less expensive players, traded Kiner in 1953. Because of back problems, he played only through 1955. He retired at age 33. Even with his career cut short, Kiner was eventually elected to the Hall of Fame.

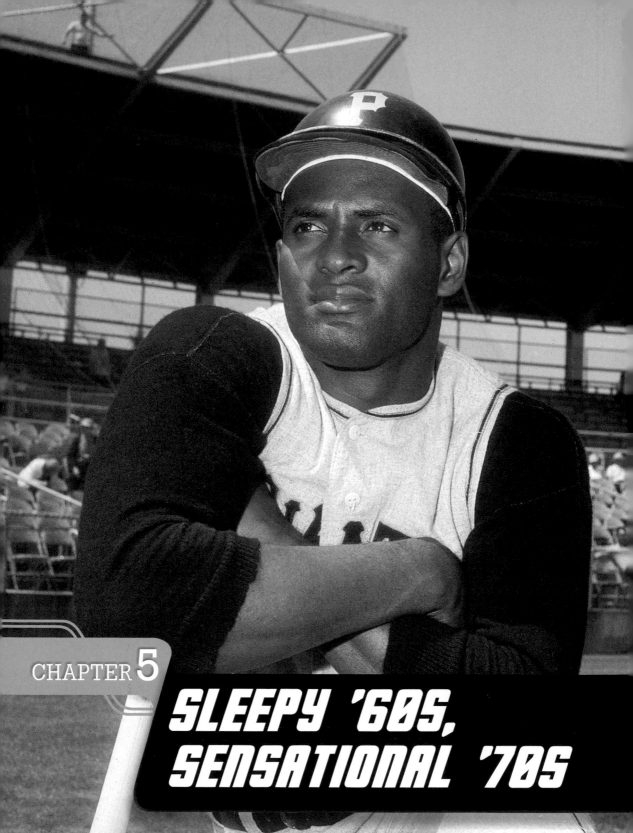

# CHAPTER 5

# SLEEPY '60S, SENSATIONAL '70S

After Bill Mazeroski's dramatic home run gave Pittsburgh the World Series title in 1960, the Pirates went into a decline. For the rest of the decade, they would not finish higher than third place.

The Pirates traded away key players from the 1960 team in an effort to improve their pitching. Shortstop Dick Groat, third baseman Don Hoak, and first baseman Dick Stuart were dealt. But the players Pittsburgh received in return did not turn the Pirates into contenders.

Even as Pittsburgh struggled, Roberto Clemente was becoming recognized as one of baseball's best players. The outfielder won four NL batting titles during the 1960s.

After the 1960s, things changed for the Pirates. First, they got a new home. In 1970, they left Forbes Field for Three Rivers Stadium. The stadium featured a playing field made up of a carpetlike artificial surface instead of grass.

Outfielder Roberto Clemente, shown in 1968, was the Pirates' biggest star in the 1960s. He was an All-Star nine times during that decade.

Steve Blass follows through after delivering a pitch in Game 7 of the 1971 World Series against host Baltimore. Blass threw a complete game, allowing just four hits, as Pittsburgh won 2–1 to capture the title.

By 1970, the Pirates had a heavy-hitting lineup nicknamed "The Lumber Company." It included Clemente, outfielder Willie Stargell, and catcher Manny Sanguillen.

In 1969, the NL and the AL reorganized into leagues with

two divisions each and began playing a round of playoffs before the World Series. The Pirates won the NL East Division in 1970. But they lost three games to none to the Cincinnati Reds in the NL Championship Series (NLCS).

Pittsburgh won the NL East again in 1971. This time, the Pirates beat the San Francisco Giants three games to one in the NLCS. Stargell had a big season. He hit 48 homers and drove in 125 runs.

In the World Series against the Baltimore Orioles, Stargell did not hit well. Clemente made up for it, though. He batted .414 against the Orioles. The Pirates also received tremendous pitching from Steve Blass. He threw two complete games, including one in the deciding 2–1 victory at Baltimore in Game 7. After 11 years, the Pirates were world champions again.

## Clemente's Legacy

*Roberto Clemente earned a huge amount of respect for how he performed on and off the baseball field. He died in a plane crash on New Year's Eve 1972, flying to bring aid to earthquake victims in Nicaragua. A few months after Clemente's death at 38, the Baseball Hall of Fame set aside its usual rules of waiting five years after a player's career for admission to the Hall. Clemente was voted into the Hall of Fame in 1973. These days, Major League Baseball's Roberto Clemente Award is "given annually to the player who combines giving back to the community with outstanding on-field skills."*

The Pirates were on a roll. They won the division again in 1972. But the Reds beat them three games to two in the NLCS.

After the season, the Pirates and their fans suffered a much greater loss. Clemente died in a plane crash in the waters off Puerto Rico. He and four other men were flying to

Nicaragua to bring supplies to earthquake victims.

After Clemente's death, the Pirates' run of first-place finishes ended. The team decided to fire manager Bill Virdon, who had won the division in 1972. Virdon was replaced by the man who had groomed him for the manager's job, Danny Murtaugh. This was Murtaugh's fourth stint as manager of the Pirates. He had led the team from 1957 to 1964, in 1967, and from 1970 to 1971.

Under Murtaugh and the man who followed him, Chuck Tanner, the Pirates were perennial contenders for the rest of the 1970s. From 1974 to 1979, Pittsburgh finished first or second every season and won the NL East three times.

The Pirates' offense benefitted from the addition of a big hitter. Outfielder Dave Parker, 6-foot-5 and 230 pounds, became a regular starting in 1975.

During the rest of the decade, Parker hit over .300 every year and won two league batting titles. He drove in at least 90 runs in four of five seasons. Parker was named NL MVP in 1978.

In the 1979 World Series, the Pirates repeated the comeback victory they had achieved in 1925. They trailed the

## "We Are Family"

*The 1979 Pirates were a championship team with a theme song. It was the hit pop song from that year titled "We Are Family." Sister Sledge was the group that sang it. The song reflected the close feelings the Pirates' players had for one another. In fact, like a family, the team's leader, slugger Willie Stargell, was called "Pops." "We are a family," Stargell said. "...I can't see living through the long season in any other way. Can you imagine what it must be like coming into a locker room with everyone pushing only for himself?"*

Pirates players, including Willie Stargell (8), celebrate after Pittsburgh defeated host Baltimore 4–1 in Game 7 of the 1979 World Series.

Orioles three games to one but won the final three games—the last two in Baltimore—to capture the championship. Pittsburgh's spiritual leader, Stargell, guided the way.

Stargell, the league co-MVP that season, hit .400 with three home runs and seven RBIs in the seven games against the Orioles.

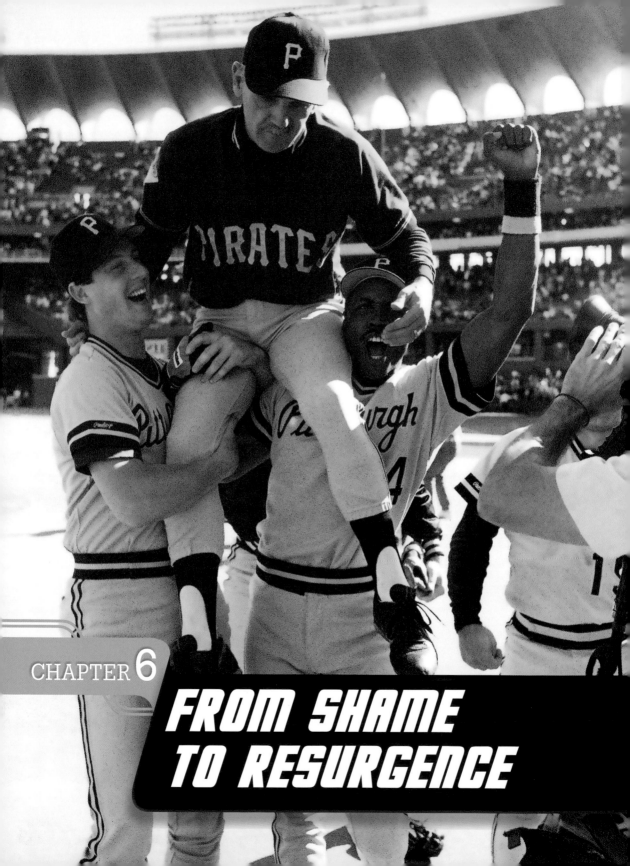

# CHAPTER 6

# FROM SHAME TO RESURGENCE

**A**s productive as the 1970s were for the Pirates, the 1980s were just the opposite. Pittsburgh did not win a division title during the decade and had six losing seasons. Attendance at Three Rivers Stadium dropped. At a time when most teams drew at least 1 million fans per season, the Pirates totaled less than 800,000 in 1984 and 1985.

Meanwhile, the owners of the Pirates, the Galbreath family, were trying to sell the team and having a hard time finding a buyer. Eventually, a group of local investors purchased the team in 1985.

However, the biggest shame involved drugs. A 1985 investigation into cocaine dealing in Pittsburgh turned up the names of several baseball players who were buying the drug. Major league players testified about their cocaine use during the trial of the drug dealers. Some were buying their drugs right at Three Rivers Stadium.

Manager Jim Leyland gets a lift from pitcher John Smiley, *left*, and outfielder Barry Bonds after the Pirates clinched the NL East title on September 30, 1990.

The most well-known Pirate among the players admitting drug use was Dave Parker. Parker and the other players did not go to jail. But Major League Baseball did fine them.

In the midst of the down years, the Pirates could point to another batting champion.

## Jim Leyland

*Jim Leyland has turned out to be one of the major leagues' most respected managers. But he had no big-league managing experience when the Pirates hired him in 1986. However, by 1992, he had put Pittsburgh in the postseason for three straight years. Leyland explained part of his philosophy this way: "All the fans expect is a good day's work. As a manager, I don't think you can ever guarantee how many wins you're going to get. I can guarantee them that our players are going to give them 100 percent, a good effort, day in and day out." After leaving the Pirates, Leyland went on to win a World Series title with the Florida Marlins in 1997 and an AL pennant with the Detroit Tigers in 2006.*

Third baseman Bill Madlock, who had joined the team in 1979, won batting titles in 1981 and 1983.

The Pirates changed managers in 1986, replacing Chuck Tanner with Jim Leyland. Though Leyland's Pirates finished last in 1986, he would lead the team to renewed success. In 1988, Pittsburgh finished second in the division. Fans were returning to Three Rivers Stadium. The Pirates set a team attendance record that year, drawing almost 1.9 million fans.

Two years later, the Pirates started a run of success. From 1990 to 1992, they won three straight NL East titles, though they lost in the NLCS each year. Twice they attracted more than 2 million fans.

The team was led by its talented outfielders. Tops among them was Barry Bonds. He was

The Pirates' Barry Bonds belts a home run in 1990 against the Cubs. Bonds had 33 homers, 114 RBIs, and 52 stolen bases that year.

a tremendous all-around player. He could hit for a high average while still producing home runs and RBIs and flashing speed on the base paths and in the outfield. Bonds was the NL's MVP in 1990 and 1992. He hit at least 25 home runs and

## BARRY BONDS

Barry Bonds ended up becoming a controversial figure. His abrasive personality had long annoyed some people, particularly members of the press.

Still, Bonds came to be recognized as baseball's best player. He could hit for power and average and was a speedy runner. Bonds was named NL MVP a record seven times—two with Pittsburgh and five while he played for the San Francisco Giants after leaving the Pirates.

While with the Giants, Bonds started hitting more home runs. He set a major league record with 73 in 2001. Bonds broke Hank Aaron's big-league record of 755 for his career, ending his career with 762 homers. Bonds became more muscular over the years. There were always rumors he had used illegal steroid drugs. Bonds never actually admitted using steroids on purpose, though. Still, many fans and members of the media believe that Bonds cheated.

collected more than 100 RBIs each season.

In 1990 and 1991, Bobby Bonilla joined Bonds in the outfield. Bonilla had 120 and 100 RBIs in those seasons. The third outfielder was Andy Van Slyke, who was not as good a hitter. However, he did bat .324 in 1992. Van Slyke was an accomplished defensive player in center field.

The pitching staff was led by Doug Drabek. He won 22 games and the NL Cy Young Award in 1990, then won 15 games in both 1991 and 1992. John Smiley won 20 for the Pirates in 1991.

Still, the Pirates failed each time in the NLCS, which had gone to a best-of-seven format by then. They lost in six games to the Cincinnati Reds in 1990, then in seven games to the Atlanta Braves in 1991 and 1992. In the playoffs,

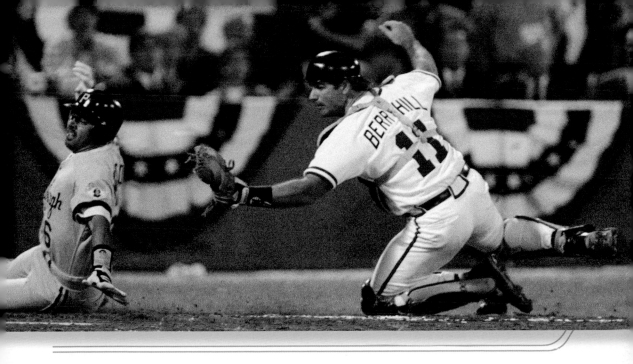

Pittsburgh's Orlando Merced tries to avoid a tag by Atlanta catcher Damon Berryhill in Game 7 of the 1992 NLCS. Merced was called out.

Bonds did not produce at all at the plate. He batted worse than .200 in 1990 and 1991 and drove in a total of three runs in the three series combined. Bonds left Pittsburgh after the 1992 season.

As of 2010, the Pirates had not returned to the playoffs.

### So Close in 1992

*The Pirates came within one out of returning to the World Series in 1992. They led the Atlanta Braves 2–1 in the bottom of the ninth inning of Game 7 of the NLCS with two outs and the bases loaded. But the Braves' Francisco Cabrera, who had batted only 10 times all season, hit a single to left field. The tying run scored. Coming from second, a slow-moving runner, Sid Bream, managed to slide across the plate with the pennant-winning run. Bream beat the throw from left fielder Barry Bonds in one of baseball's most memorable moments.*

# CHAPTER 7

# DOWN YEARS

After a third straight division title in 1992, the Pirates started a streak of down seasons. Through 2010, they had not been back to the postseason. The Pirates had not posted a winning record since 1992. In 2001 and 2010, they lost 100 and 105 games, respectively.

In one year, 1997, they stayed in contention for the NL Central Division title until the season's last weekend. (The league had split into three divisions starting in 1994.) But even in that season, the Pirates finished with a losing record.

The Pirates' decline coincided with the departure of star outfielder Barry Bonds.

## Staying Put

In 1996, with the Pirates losing money and up for sale, Pittsburgh fans were afraid the team could be moving. It seemed no local group was able to buy the Pirates. Buyers from out of town might have wanted to put the Pirates in another city. But a group led by Kevin McClatchy bought the team. Though McClatchy was not from Pittsburgh, he kept the Pirates in Pittsburgh.

Andrew McCutchen, shown in 2010, played well again in his second major league season, but the Pirates posted their 18th losing year in a row.

He left Pittsburgh after the 1992 season. Bonds signed as a free agent with the San Francisco Giants. The Pirates' best pitcher, Doug Drabek, also left. He signed with the Houston Astros after 1992.

The Pirates still had some bright moments, though. On July 12, 1997, Francisco Cordova pitched nine no-hit innings and Ricardo Rincon added another, and the Pirates defeated the Astros 3–0 on Mark Smith's home run in the bottom of the 10th inning. It was the first combined, extra-inning no-hitter in major league history.

In 2000, the Pirates played their last season at Three Rivers Stadium. In 2001, they moved into their new stadium, PNC Park. Pittsburgh lost 100 games but still drew a club-record 2.4 million fans.

Third baseman Freddy Sanchez won the NL batting

## Roberto Clemente Bridge

In 1999, the Sixth Street Bridge in Pittsburgh was renamed the Roberto Clemente Bridge in honor of the late Pirates Hall of Fame outfielder. The bridge goes over the Allegheny River near PNC Park. When the Pirates are playing at home, the bridge is closed to vehicles so fans can walk to and from the ballpark over the bridge.

title in 2006. He hit .344. But Sanchez was traded to the Giants in 2009. He was one of several talented Pirates to leave the team during the long streak of losing seasons.

Outfielder Jason Bay was NL Rookie of the Year in 2004. He followed that up with All-Star seasons in 2005 and 2006, when he drove in more than 100 runs each year. But Bay was part of a trade in 2008 that sent him to the Boston Red Sox. In his first full season as the Pirates' starting third baseman

PNC Park is shown on March 31, 2001, during a Pirates exhibition game against the Mets that opened Pittsburgh's new stadium.

in 2001, Aramis Ramirez had 34 homers and 112 RBIs. His statistics declined in 2002. The Pirates traded him to the Cubs in 2003. With Chicago, Ramirez drove in more than 100 runs in four more seasons.

Center fielder Andrew McCutchen emerged with an outstanding rookie season in 2009 for Pittsburgh. He continued to play well in 2010, even as the team struggled badly. Fans hope that the tradition-rich Pirates can someday soon put together a roster that has more players like McCutchen and finally become contenders again.

# TIMELINE

|  |  |
|------|-------|
| **1876** | The Pittsburgh Alleghenys play as the city's first professional baseball team. |
| **1891** | The Pittsburgh club signs second baseman Louis Bierbauer and is accused of stealing him from another team. When the club is referred to as "pirates," the name sticks. |
| **1900** | When the NL cuts the number of teams from 12 to eight, the owner of the closed-down Louisville team, Barney Dreyfuss, takes over as owner of the Pirates. Among the 14 players Dreyfuss brings with him is shortstop Honus Wagner. |
| **1903** | The NL champion Pirates agree to meet the champions of the AL, the Boston Americans, in the first World Series. Boston wins the Series five games to three. |
| **1909** | The Pirates open Forbes Field. They return to the World Series and defeat the Detroit Tigers for the championship. Wagner outplays Tigers great Ty Cobb. |
| **1925** | Pittsburgh wins the NL and takes on the Washington Senators, featuring the great pitcher Walter Johnson, in the World Series. The Pirates capture the title by becoming the first team ever to come back from a three-games-to-one deficit. |
| **1927** | The Pirates reach the World Series again but fall in four straight games to the mighty New York Yankees. Pittsburgh will not return to the World Series until 1960. |
| **1946** | Ralph Kiner joins the Pirates as a rookie and wins the first of a record seven straight NL home-run titles. |

| 1960 | The Pirates win the NL pennant and then defeat the Yankees in the World Series. Pittsburgh wins Game 7 on October 13 at Forbes Field on a homer by Bill Mazeroski. |

| 1970 | Pittsburgh begins playing at Three Rivers Stadium. The Pirates win the first of three straight NL East titles. |

| 1971 | Led by Roberto Clemente, the Pirates defeat the Baltimore Orioles in the World Series. Clemente hits a solo homer and Steve Blass pitches a complete game as Pittsburgh wins 2–1 in Game 7 on October 17 at Baltimore. |

| 1979 | The Pirates, famous for their "We Are Family" theme song, play the Orioles again in the World Series. Pittsburgh trails in the Series three games to one before winning Games 5, 6, and 7 for the championship. Willie Stargell goes 4-for-5 with a two-run homer to help visiting Pittsburgh prevail 4–1 in Game 7 on October 17. |

| 1992 | The Pirates win the NL East a third consecutive year, but the Atlanta Braves beat Pittsburgh four games to three in the NLCS. It is the third straight year that the Pirates fall in the NLCS. Pittsburgh left fielder Barry Bonds wins his second NL MVP honor. The first came in 1990. |

| 1996 | Kevin McClatchy leads a group that buys the Pirates and keeps them in Pittsburgh. |

| 2001 | The Pirates play their first regular-season game at PNC Park, falling 8–2 to the Cincinnati Reds on April 9. |

| 2009 | Center fielder Andrew McCutchen finishes fourth in the NL Rookie of the Year voting after batting .286 with 12 homers, 54 RBIs, and 22 stolen bases in 108 games. |

# QUICK STATS

## FRANCHISE HISTORY

Pittsburgh Alleghenys
(1882–90)
Pittsburgh Pirates
(1891– )

## WORLD SERIES
*(wins in bold)*

1903, **1909**, **1925**, 1927, **1960**, **1971**, **1979**

## NL CHAMPIONSHIP SERIES
*(1969– )*

1970, 1971, 1972, 1974, 1975, 1979, 1990, 1991, 1992

## DIVISION CHAMPIONSHIPS
*(1969– )*

1970, 1971, 1972, 1974, 1975, 1979, 1990, 1991, 1992

## KEY PLAYERS
*(position[s]; seasons with team)*

Barry Bonds (OF; 1986–92)
Max Carey (OF; 1910–26)
Roberto Clemente (OF; 1955–72)
Ralph Kiner (OF; 1946–53)
Bill Mazeroski (2B; 1956–72)
Dave Parker (OF; 1973–83)
Willie Stargell (OF/1B; 1962–82)
Pie Traynor (3B; 1920–35, 1937)
Honus Wagner (SS; 1900–17)
Lloyd Waner (OF; 1927–41, 1944–45)
Paul Waner (OF; 1926–40)

## KEY MANAGERS

Fred Clarke (1900–15):
    1,422–969; 7–8 (postseason)
Bill McKechnie (1922–26):
    409–293; 4–3 (postseason)
Danny Murtaugh (1957–64, 1967,
    1970–71, 1973–76):
    1,115–950; 12–16 (postseason)

## HOME PARKS

Exposition Park I (1882–83)
Recreation Park (1884–90)
Exposition Park II (1891–1909)
Forbes Field (1909–70)
Three Rivers Stadium (1970–2000)
PNC Park (2001– )

\* All statistics through 2010 season

# QUOTES AND ANECDOTES

When Barney Dreyfuss owned the Pirates, he would offer to invest his players' money in the stock market at no risk to them. He would deduct part of their salaries to invest, and they would get any profits the stocks made. But he also would pay them back if the stocks lost money.

"We found a different way to lose every night. It was exciting. A fly ball would go up, and we didn't know who was going to catch it or if somebody was going to catch it."
—Joe Garagiola, catcher on the awful 1952 Pirates

*I won't tell no lie*
*All of the people around us they say*
*Can they be that close*
*Just let me state for the record*
*We're giving love in a family dose*
—Lyrics from "We Are Family," the Pirates' theme song in 1979

Relief pitcher Kent Tekulve was one of the most recognizable Pirates in the 1970s and 1980s. The right-hander wore tinted glasses and threw in a "submarine," or underhand, style. The pitching motion was unusual but effective. It made hitters uncomfortable and allowed Tekulve to pitch more frequently than most hurlers because he put less stress on his arm. Tekulve made his debut with the Pirates in 1974. He led the major leagues in games pitched three times (91 in 1978, 94 in 1979, and 85 in 1982) with Pittsburgh. He had 31 saves in 1978 and the same number again in 1979. He saved three games in the 1979 World Series, including the Game 7 clincher. He played with Pittsburgh until 1985, when he was traded to Philadelphia.

# GLOSSARY

**accomplished**

Having achieved great things.

**acquire**

To receive a player through trade or by signing as a free agent.

**attendance**

The number of fans at a particular game or who come to watch a team play during a particular season.

**contender**

A team that is considered good enough to win a championship.

**distinctive**

Unique, not like any other.

**franchise**

An entire sports organization, including the players, coaches, and staff.

**free agent**

A player whose contract has expired and who is able to sign with a team of his choice.

**general manager**

The executive who is in charge of the team's overall operation. He or she hires and fires managers and coaches, drafts players, and signs free agents.

**ill-fated**

Doomed to fail.

**pennant**

A flag. In baseball, it symbolizes that a team has won its league championship.

**postseason**

Games played in the playoffs by the top teams after the regular-season schedule has been completed.

**press box**

Part of a stadium where reporters sit to cover a game.

**roster**

The players as a whole on a baseball team.

# *FOR MORE INFORMATION*

## Further Reading

Perdomo, Willie. *Clemente!* New York: Henry Holt and Co., 2010.

Reisler, Jim. *The Best Game Ever: Pirates 10, Yankees 9: October 13, 1960.* Cambridge, MA: Da Capo Press, 2009.

Smizik, Bob. *The Pittsburgh Pirates: An Illustrated History.* New York: Walker & Company, 1990.

## Web Links

To learn more about the Pittsburgh Pirates, visit ABDO Publishing Company online at **www.abdopublishing.com**. Web sites about the Pirates are featured on our Book Links page. These links are routinely monitored and updated to provide the most current information available.

## Places to Visit

### National Baseball Hall of Fame and Museum

25 Main Street
Cooperstown, NY 13326
1-888-HALL-OF-FAME
www.baseballhall.org
This hall of fame and museum highlights the greatest players and moments in the history of baseball. Roberto Clemente, Willie Stargell, and Honus Wagner are among the former Pirates enshrined here.

### PNC Park

115 Federal Street
Pittsburgh, PA 15212
412-323-5000
mlb.mlb.com/pit/ballpark/index.jsp
This has been the Pirates' home field since 2001. The team plays 81 regular-season games here each year.

### Western Pennsylvania Sports Museum

1212 Smallman Street
Pittsburgh, PA 15222
412-454-6000
www.heinzhistorycenter.org/sportsMuseum.aspx
This museum has exhibits about all sorts of sports and teams from the region, including the Pirates.

# INDEX

## About the Author

Ray Frager is a freelance writer based in the Baltimore, Maryland, area. He has been a professional sports editor and writer since 1980. He has worked for the *Trenton Times*, the *Dallas Morning News*, the *Baltimore Sun*, and FOXSports.com. At the *Sun*, he edited books on Cal Ripken Jr., the building of Baltimore's football stadium, and the Baltimore Ravens' 2000 Super Bowl season.